My Song Is Beautiful

Poems and Pictures in Many Voices

Selected by
Mary Ann Hoberman

Little, Brown and Company
Boston   New York   Toronto   London

In memory of Jesse Murry

First Edition

Acknowledgments • Thanks are given as follows for permission to reprint copyrighted material: **Mary Austin:** "A Song of Greatness" from *The Children Sing in the Far West,* by Mary Austin. Copyright 1928 by Mary Austin. Copyright © renewed 1956 by Kenneth M. Chapman and Mary C. Wheelwright. Reprinted by permission of Houghton Mifflin Company. All rights reserved. **Toni de Gerez:** "My Song" from *My Song Is a Piece of Jade: Poems of Ancient Mexico in English and Spanish,* adapted by Toni de Gerez. English translation copyright © 1984 by Organización Editorial Novaro S.A. Reprinted by permission of Little, Brown and Company. **Nikki Giovanni:** "the drum" from *Spin a Soft Black Song,* by Nikki Giovanni. Copyright © 1971, 1985 by Nikki Giovanni. Reprinted by permission of Farrar, Straus & Giroux, Inc. **Nicole Hernandez:** "No Shadow in the Water" copyright © 1992 by Nicole Hernandez. Reprinted by permission of the author. **Felice Holman:** "Who Am I?" from *At the Top of My Voice and Other Poems,* by Felice Holman. Copyright © 1970 by Felice Holman. Reprinted by permission of the author. **James Houston:** "Ayii, Ayii, Ayii" (Central Eskimo) from *Songs of the Dream People,* edited and illustrated by James Houston. Copyright © 1972 by James Houston. Reprinted by permission of James Houston. **Langston Hughes:** "Birth" from *Fields of Wonder,* by Langston Hughes. Copyright © 1974 by Langston Hughes. Reprinted by permission of Alfred A. Knopf, Inc. **Ruth Krauss:** "Beginning on Paper" reprinted by permission of the author. **Karla Kuskin:** "Me" from *Dogs & Dragons, Trees & Dreams,* by Karla Kuskin. Copyright © 1980 by Karla Kuskin. Reprinted by permission of HarperCollins Publishers. **A. A. Milne:** "The End" from *Now We Are Six,* by A. A. Milne. Copyright 1927 by E. P. Dutton, © renewed 1955 by A. A. Milne. Reprinted by permission of Dutton Children's Books, a division of Penguin Books USA Inc. (U.S., Canada, Philippines), and Methuen Children's Books (U.K.). **Jack Prelutsky:** "Me I Am" from *The Random House Book of Poetry for Children,* selected and introduced by Jack Prelutsky. Copyright © 1983 by Jack Prelutsky. Reprinted by permission of Random House, Inc. **Michael Rosen:** "I Know Someone" from *Quick, Let's Get Out of Here,* by Michael Rosen. Copyright © 1984 by Michael Rosen. Reprinted by permission of Scholastic Publications Ltd. **Kim Soo-Jang:** "In a Hermit's Cottage" by Kim Soo-Jang, from *Sunset in a Spider Web,* adapted by Virginia Olsen Baron. Copyright © 1974 by Virginia Olsen Baron. Reprinted by permission of Henry Holt and Company, Inc., and Virginia Olsen Baron.

Library of Congress Cataloging-in-Publication Data
My song is beautiful : poems and pictures in many voices /
selected by Mary Ann Hoberman. — 1st ed.
p.   cm.
ISBN 0-316-36738-9
1. Children's poetry. [1. Poetry — Collections.] I. Hoberman, Mary Ann.
PN6109.97.M9   1994
808.81'0083 — dc20   93-24976

10 9 8 7 6 5 4 3 2 1

SC

Published simultaneously in Canada by Little, Brown & Company (Canada) Limited

Printed in Hong Kong

CONTENTS

MY SONG

A Toltec Poem from Ancient Mexico

Like the feathers
of the quetzal bird
my song is beautiful

Now look!

My song is bending over
           the earth

My song is born
in the house of butterflies

Translated by Toni de Gerez

BIRTH

Oh, fields of wonder
Out of which
Stars are born,
And moon and sun
And me as well,
Like stroke
Of lightning
In the night
Some mark
To make
Some word
To tell.

— *Langston Hughes*

BEGINNING ON PAPER

on paper
I write it
on rain

I write it
on stones
on my boots

on trees
I write it
on the air

on the city
how pretty
I write my name

— *Ruth Krauss*

ME

"My nose is blue,
My teeth are green,
My face is like a soup tureen.
I look just like a lima bean.
I'm very, very lovely.
My feet are far too short
And long.
My hands are left and right
And wrong.
My voice is like the hippo's song.
I'm very, very,
Very, very,
Very, very
Lovely?"

— *Karla Kuskin*

THE DRUM

daddy says the world is
a drum tight and hard
and i told him
i'm gonna beat
out my own rhythm

— *Nikki Giovanni*

A SONG OF GREATNESS
A Chippewa Indian Song

When I hear the old men
Telling of heroes,
Telling of great deeds
Of ancient days,
When I hear them telling,
Then I think within me
I too am one of these.

When I hear the people
Praising great ones,
Then I know that I too
Shall be esteemed,
I too when my time comes
Shall do mightily.

Translated by Mary Austin

ME I AM!

I am the only ME I AM
who qualifies as me;
no ME I AM has been before,
and none will ever be.

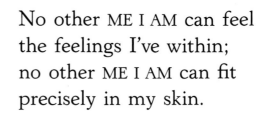

No other ME I AM can feel
the feelings I've within;
no other ME I AM can fit
precisely in my skin.

There is no other ME I AM
who thinks the thoughts I do;
the world contains one ME I AM,
there is no room for two.

I am the only ME I AM
this earth shall ever see;
that ME I AM I always am
is no one else but ME!

— *Jack Prelutsky*

I KNOW SOMEONE

I know someone who can
take a mouthful of custard and blow it
down their nose.

I know someone who can
make their ears wiggle.
I know someone who can
shake their cheeks so it sounds
like ducks quacking.

I know someone who can
throw peanuts in the air and catch them
in their mouth.

I know someone who can
balance a pile of 12 pennies on his elbow
and snatch his elbow from under them
and catch them.

I know someone who can
bend her thumb back to touch her wrist.

I know someone who can
crack his nose.
I know someone who can
say the alphabet backwards.

I know someone who can put their hands in
their armpits and blow raspberries.

I know someone who can
wiggle her little toe.

I know someone who can
lick the bottom of her chin.

I know someone who can
slide their top lip one way
and their bottom lip the other way.
And that someone is

ME.

— *Michael Rosen*

AYII, AYII, AYII
A Central Eskimo Chant

Ayii, ayii, ayii,
My arms, they wave high in the air,
My hands, they flutter behind my back,
They wave above my head
Like the wings of a bird.
Let me move my feet.
Let me dance.
Let me shrug my shoulders.
Let me shake my body.
Let me crouch down.
My arms, let me fold them.
Let me hold my hands under my chin.

Translated by James Houston

NO SHADOW IN THE WATER

I see myself
in the water
and my face
is shining
down
deep.

— *Nicole Hernandez*

Carol Palmer

YOU AND I

Only one I in the whole wide world
And millions and millions of you,
But every you is an I to itself
And I am a you to you, too!

But if I am a you and you are an I
And the opposite also is true,
It makes us both the same somehow
Yet splits us each in two.

It's more and more mysterious,
The more I think it through:
Every you everywhere in the world is an I;
Every I in the world is a you!

— *Mary Ann Hoberman*

IN A HERMIT'S COTTAGE

In a hermit's cottage, silent, still,
I sit all alone with nobody.
A white cloud dozes
To the strains of a quiet song.

No one can know
How happy I am!

— Kim Soo-Jang
Translated by Virginia Olsen Baron

WHO AM I?

The trees ask me,
And the sky,
And the sea asks me
  Who am I?

The grass asks me,
And the sand,
And the rocks ask me
  Who am I?

The wind tells me
At nightfall,
And the rain tells me
  Someone small.

  Someone small
  Someone small
  But a piece
    of
    it
    all.

 — *Felice Holman*

THE END

When I was One,
I had just begun.

When I was Two,
I was nearly new.

When I was Three,
I was hardly Me.

When I was Four,
I was not much more.

When I was Five,
I was just alive.

But now I am Six, I'm as clever as clever.
So I think I'll be six now for ever and ever.

— *A. A. Milne*

NOTES ON THE POETS AND ARTISTS

Andrea Arroyo is a Mexican artist whose work appears regularly in *The New Yorker* and the *New York Times*. Her illustration is in watercolor and ink on paper.

Mary Austin (1868–1934) was a writer committed to the preservation of Native American folklore. She translated the poem here from Chippewa.

Ashley Bryan has produced several brilliantly illustrated retellings of African folktales, including *Beat the Story-Drum, Pum-Pum,* which won the Coretta Scott King Award. His painting is in tempera and gouache.

Dale DeArmond has published many books based on the mythology of the native people of Alaska, her home. Her piece is a wood engraving cut in an end-grain maple block and printed in a manually operated etching press.

Toni de Gerez has lived all over Latin America, lecturing and writing on native mythology and verse. She translated the poem included here, which was sung in magical ceremonies by the Toltec people of ancient Mexico, from the original Náhuatl language.

Catherine De Vuono, an artist-instructor for New York City's Studio in a School program, guided elementary students from Brooklyn P.S. 16 in creating the self-portrait quilt featured here, which is composed of painted fabric, stitch-sewn together. The young artists who contributed to this piece are: F. Davis, J. Negron, K. Pagan, A. Guzzman, C. Seetram, A. Fowler, N. Salim, E. Shafidiya, T. Jie, B. Rahaman, M. Resto, and M. Bayne.

David Diaz's artwork is a silk-screen print to which watercolors have been applied. He is the illustrator of *Neighborhood Odes.*

Bernie Fuchs's painting was done in oil on canvas. The illustrator of the highly acclaimed picture book *Ragtime Tumpie,* he has received over one hundred awards for his work.

Nikki Giovanni is one of the most well-known figures of the New Black Poetry and has written many books, including *Spin a Soft Black Song.*

Nicole Hernandez is a seventh-grader at Junior High School 126 in Brooklyn. This is her first published poem.

Mary Ann Hoberman wrote her poem "You and I" especially for this anthology, of which she is also the editor.

Felice Holman published her first children's book, *Elizabeth, The Bird Watcher,* thirty years ago and has since written almost twenty additional books for children.

James Houston lived in the arctic among the Eskimo people for fourteen years, recording their songs and stories in collections such as *Songs of the Dream People.*

Langston Hughes (1902–1967) was a celebrated African-American poet and writer whose many books include *The Dream Keeper.*

Yoriko Ito was born and raised in Mie, Japan, and now lives and works in San Francisco. Her piece was done in acrylic and mixed media.

Elisa Kleven is self-taught and works in a mixed-media collage technique, reminiscent of the way she used and compiled materials in her childhood creations. She is the illustrator of *Abuela.*

Ruth Krauss (1901–1993) is the author of the classic children's books *The Carrot Seed* and *A Hole Is to Dig.*

Karla Kuskin is an award-winning poet whose collections include *Dogs and Dragons, Trees and Dreams.*

David McPhail has created more than forty picture books, including his most recent, *Santa's Book of Names.* His illustration was done in pen-and-ink and watercolor.

Holly Meade used a combination of silk-screen printing and gouache painting to create her piece. She is the illustrator of *Rata-Pata-Scata-Fata.*

Susan Meddaugh's art is a combination of pen-and-ink, watercolor, and colored pencils. She is the creator of *Martha Speaks,* a *New York Times* Best Illustrated book.

A. A. Milne (1882–1956) is best known for his beloved Winnie-the-Pooh books as well as his several collections of verse for children.

Keiko Narahashi's artwork is in watercolor. Her latest book is *The Magic Purse,* a Japanese folktale by Yoshiko Uchida.

Carol Palmer hand-tints her black-and-white photographs. She often exhibits her pictures of children and their families in New England.

Jack Prelutsky has over thirty volumes of poetry collections to his name. He frequently presents poems to children in schools and libraries.

Michael Rosen is both a poet and a storyteller and has written many popular books for young readers, including *Don't Put the Mustard in the Custard.*

Irana Shepherd's illustration was created with a combination of watercolor, gouache, and pastel. She illustrated *Bronco Dogs.*

Kim Soo-Jang's poem is a Sijo poem, one of the earliest and most popular forms of Korean verse. It has been translated by Virginia Olsen Baron, the editor of several anthologies of Asian poetry.